LIVING THINGS

PRAYING MANTIS

Rebecca Stefoff

BENCHMARK BOOKS
MARSHALL CAVENDISH
NEW YORK

Benchmark Books
Marshall Cavendish Corporation
99 White Plains Road
Tarrytown, New York 10591-9001

Illustrations by Jean Cassels

Library of Congress Cataloging-in-Publication Data
Stefoff, Rebecca, date
Praying Mantis / by Rebecca Stefoff.
p. cm. — (Living things)
Includes bibliographical references and index.
Summary: Introduces the life cycle and habitat of the praying mantis
as well as the related stick and leaf insects.
ISBN 0-7614-0120-2 (lib. bdg.)
1. Praying mantis—Juvenile literature. [1. Praying mantis.]
I. Title. II. Series: Stefoff, Rebecca, date Living things.
QL508.M4S74 1997 595.7'25—dc20 96-18482 CIP AC

Photo research by Ellen Barrett Dudley

Cover photo: *Photo Researchers, Inc.*, Dr. Paul A. Zahl

The photographs in this book are used by permission and through the courtesy of *Animals Animals:* Richard Kolar, 2; Michael Fogden/Oxford Scientific Films, 13; K.G. Preston Mafham, 16 (right), 17 (bottom), 25, 27; Bob Fredrick/Oxford Scientific Films, 17 (top); Stephen Dalton, 22 (right); Karen Tweedy-Holmes, 26; David G. Fox/Oxford Scientific Films, 32. *Photo Researchers:* Steve Maslowski, 6; Darwin Dale, 7; Harold R. Hungerford, 8; Louis Quilt, 9 (left); Michael Lustbader, 9 (right); Dr. Paul A. Zahl, 10; Simon D. Pollard, 11; Gary Retherford, 12 (left), 19; M.P. Kahl, 12 (right); Andrew Martinez, 14; Nuridsany Perennou, 15; E.R. Degginger, 18 (top); Biophoto Association, 18 (bottom); Ray Coleman, 20 (right); Danny Brass, 21; Jeffrey W. Lang, 22 (left); Jacana, 23; John Mitchell, 24. *Tom Stack and Associates:* Joe McDonald, 16 (left). *Peter Arnold:* John MacGregor, 20 (left).

Printed in the United States of America

5 6 4

For my father

Chinese mantis, Ohio

PRAYING MANTIS

praying mantis

Yikes! What's that scary-looking green thing with the big eyes and long, waving feelers?

Don't be afraid. It's not a monster. It's only a praying mantis — a strange and wonderful insect.

See how the praying mantis sits with its front legs neatly folded? People sometimes fold their hands in front of them when they pray. That's how the praying mantis got its name.

praying mantis, Illinois

mantis's front leg

praying mantis, New York

The mantis uses its front legs to grab other insects. The sharp spines on the mantis's legs hold the insects in place while the mantis eats them.

The mantis sees very well with its big eyes. And it can turn its head to look over its own shoulder. If you walk past a praying mantis, it will turn its head to watch you.

mantis eating grasshopper

Mantises are fierce hunters. They attack stinging wasps, poisonous spiders, and other mantises. Some mantises even attack small birds and mice.

The only insect mantises don't like to eat is ants. Even if a mantis is very hungry, it won't touch an ant. Nobody knows why.

mantis eating jumping spider

empusa mantis, France

grizzled mantis, Florida

Mantises that live in green plants are green. Mantises that live on gray tree bark are gray. And mantises that live in pink flowers — well, you can guess what color they are.

Blending into their background helps mantises hide. The mantises catch their food by sitting very still until an insect passes by. Then they leap out of hiding and snatch their prey.

slender flower mantis, Malaysia

praying mantis, New Hampshire

mantis, Saudi Arabia

There are about eighteen hundred different kinds of mantises in the world. No matter how different they look, all mantises are alike in some ways. All of them have six legs, big eyes, and heads shaped like triangles.

leaf mantis, Ecuador

flower mantis, Africa

Some of the strangest mantises live in the tropical rain forests.

They look like the leaves and flowers of jungle plants.

A few mantises have big spots on their backs. When the mantises spread their wings, the spots look like eyes. What a surprise for any animal or bird that is thinking about eating that mantis! The surprise gives the mantis a chance to get away.

eyed mantis, Africa

flower mantis, Africa

wandering leaf insect, Malaysia

tropical stick insect

The mantis's closest relatives are the leaf and stick insects.

Leaf insects look like brown or green leaves. They fasten themselves to plants and sway in the breeze, just like leaves.

Stick insects are long and narrow, like little sticks. A few stick insects look like they have fuzzy moss growing on them.

Most leaf and stick insects live in the tropics. But some stick insects live in the United States. Perhaps you'll see one someday, hiding among twigs or grass.

stick insect, Costa Rica

The mantis begins life in an egg case, a tough shell about the size of a big grape. Through the winter, the eggs lie safe in the case.

When spring comes, tiny baby mantises called nymphs crawl out of the case. Each nymph is about the size of a mosquito.

The nymphs hurry to explore the outside world. The little hunters are hungry for their first meal.

mantis egg case

nymphs leaving egg case

newly hatched praying mantis, New York

immature mantis, New Guinea

praying mantis in flight

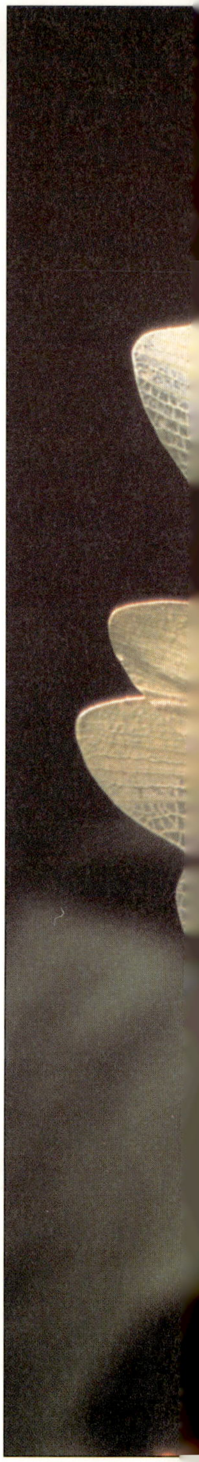

It takes all summer for a young mantis to reach its full size. At first the mantis can't fly. Its wings are too short. Later the wings get bigger, and the mantis can fly. But it would rather sit and wait for food to come to it.

When something scares a mantis, it spreads its wings and rears up on its back legs. This is how the mantis says, "Leave me alone."

mantis in threatening pose

mantises mating

At the end of the summer the grown-up mantises are ready to have babies. Now the father mantis mates with the mother. But he must be very careful. Hungry mother mantises sometimes turn around and eat the fathers.

female mantis laying eggs in egg case

Next the mother mantis spins an egg case and fills it with a hundred or more eggs. At first the egg case is white and as soft as whipped cream. In just a few hours, it will turn brown. Then it will be as hard as a peanut shell.

nymphs leaving egg case

For months the eggs have waited in the case. Now it is spring, and the nymphs climb out of the case. They run in all directions, ready for a season of growing and hunting. In the fall they will be ready to have babies of their own.

young mantises, Trinidad

A QUICK LOOK AT THE PRAYING MANTIS

Praying mantises belong to a group of insects called mantids. Some of their closest relatives, the stick and leaf insects, are also mantids. The rest of the stick and leaf insects belong to another group of insects called phasmids. There are more than four thousand different kinds of mantids and phasmids in the world. Most of them live in tropical areas.

Here are six kinds of mantids and phasmids, along with their scientific names in Latin and a few key facts.

PRAYING MANTIS

Mantis religiosa

(MAN tiss reh lih gee OH sah)

Name dates from 1758 and refers to mantis's appearance of "praying" with folded hands. Originally found only in southern Europe, but now common in the United States and southern Canada. Tan when young, bright green in adult form.

DEAD-LEAF MANTIS

Acanthops falcata

(ah CAN tops fahl KAH tah)

Lives in tropical rain forests in Central and South America. Females have no wings. Both males and females are shaped and colored like dead leaves to help them hide in vegetation.

AFRICAN FLOWER MANTIS

Harpagomantis discolor

(har pah goh MAN tiss DISS koh lor)

Native to South Africa. Colored pink and green to blend into background of flowers. Frilly growths on the body look like flower petals, helping the mantis hide among blooms.

WANDERING LEAF INSECT

Phyllium Bioculatum

(FILL yum bye oh cue LAY tum)

Belongs to the phasmid group of insects. Lives in tropical Southeast Asia. Flat green or brown body looks like a leaf. Sometimes sways or moves to look like a leaf blowing in the breeze.

ASIAN FLOWER MANTIS

Hymenopus coronatus

(hi MEH noh puhs coh roh NAY tus)

One of the world's rarest mantids, found in the Southeast Asian countries of Malaysia and Indonesia. Bright pink, with petal-shaped legs and wings. Hides among pink jungle flowers.

CHINESE MANTIS
Tenodera aridifolia sinensis
(tenn oh DEH rah ah rih dih FOHL yah see NEN sis)
Originally found in many parts of eastern Asia. Now common in the United States, where it is the largest mantis, about 4 inches long (10 cm). Sometimes used by gardeners to devour insect pests.

Taking Care of the Praying Mantis

Praying mantises and their relatives, the stick and the leaf insects, help farmers and gardeners by eating bugs that can harm crops and flowers. Now we can help the mantises. We need to protect tropical rain forests, woodlands, and grassy fields so that the praying mantises will always have a home.

Find Out More

Earle, Olive. *Praying Mantis.* New York: Morrow, 1969.

Hess, Lilo. *The Praying Mantis: Insect Cannibal.* New York: Scribner, 1971.

Johnson, Sylvia A. *Mantises.* Minneapolis: Lerner Publications, 1984.

Lavies, Bianca. *Backyard Hunter: The Praying Mantis.* New York: Dutton, 1990.

Index

Rebecca Stefoff has published many books for young readers. Science and environmental issues are among her favorite subjects. She lives in Oregon and enjoys observing the natural world while hiking, camping, and scuba diving.

praying mantis, Portugal